The
Ulster
RECITER

Edited by
Joe McPartland

Designed by
Maria Holland

THE
BLACKSTAFF
PRESS

First published in 1984 by
The Blackstaff Press Limited
3 Galway Park, Dundonald, Belfast BT16 2AN, Northern Ireland
Reprinted 1985, 1987, 1988, 1989, 1990, 1992, 1994, 1998

Printed by The Guernsey Press Company Limited

British Library Cataloguing in Publication Data
The Ulster Reciter
1. Ballads, English
I. McPartland, Joe
821'.044'08 PR1181

ISBN 0-85640-321-0

CONTENTS

Favourite Imports

FOREWORD

One of the most significant traits in the Ulster character is the willingness – indeed insistence at times – to stand up and recite at the drop of a bowler hat. And there isn't a pub or a club in the province that doesn't have its memories of the man or woman who recited 'The Ballad of William Bloat' or 'The Ould Orange Flute'.

In some of the most unlikely places you will hear 'The Man from God Knows Where' to say nothing of that sweet innocent 'The Hottest Wee Widow in Larne'. It's the nature of the place – and there is always an audience for the man or woman who can bring a tear to the eye or a laugh to the proceedings. In this collection I have gathered a number of my own special favourites and, in response to those who can always remember a line or a verse, but never the whole, I have included many other poems. The range is wide – mainly local products, but also favourite imports – from Percy French, Padraig Gregory and Padraic Colum to Rudyard Kipling and Robert Service. W.F. Marshall and Raymond Calvert are included and, of course, the greatest poet in the language, our old friend 'Anon'.

I hope readers (and listeners) will get from the collection some of the enjoyment that went into its preparation. I've heard all these ballads and poems recited in Ulster at one time or another and, indeed, have been persuaded on numerous occasions to recite many of them myself – at the drop of a bowler hat.

Special thanks to Nellie Bell, Tom Goyer, John Killen and his colleagues at the Linen Hall Library, the staff of Belfast Central Library and everyone else who came forward with ideas, even if their favourite was not finally included in the collection.

Joe McPartland, 1984

The Man From God Knows Where

NTO our townlan', on a night of snow,
Rode a man from God-knows-where;
None of us bade him stay or go,
Nor deemed him friend, nor damned him foe,
But we stabled his big roan mare:
For in our townlan' we're a decent folk,
And if he didn't speak, why none of us spoke,
And we sat till the fire burned low.

We're a civil sort in our wee place;
So we made the circle wide
Round Andy Lemon's cheerful blaze,
And wished the man his length o' days,
And a good end to his ride,
He smiled in under his slouchy hat –
Says he: 'There's a bit of a joke in that,
For we ride different ways.'

The whiles we smoked we watched him stare,
From his seat fornenst the glow.
I nudged Joe Moore, 'You wouldn't dare
To ask him, who he's for meeting there,
And how far he has got to go.'
But Joe wouldn't dare, nor Wully Scott,
And he took no drink – neither cold nor hot –
This man from God-knows-where.

It was closin' time an' late forbye,
When us ones braved the air –
I never saw worse (may I live or die)
Than the sleet that night, an' I says, says I,
'You'll find he's for stoppin' there.'
But at skreek o' day, through the gable pane,
I watched him spur in the peltin' rain,
And I juked from his rovin' eye.

Well, 'twas gettin' on past the heat o' the year
When I rode to Newtown fair:
I sold as I could (the dealers were near —
Only three pounds eight for the Innish steer,
An' nothin' at all for the mare!)
I met McKee in the throng o' the street,
Says he, 'The grass has grown under our feet
Since they hanged young Warwick here.'

And he told me that Boney had promised help
To a man in Dublin town.
Says he, 'If ye've laid the pike on the shelf,
Ye'd better go home hot-fut by yerself,
An' once more take it down.'
So by Comber Road I trotted the gray
And never cut corn until Killyleagh
Stood plain on the rising groun'.

For a wheen o' days we sat waitin' the word
To rise and go at it like men.
But no French ships sailed into Cloughey Bay,
And we heard the black news on a harvest day
That the cause was lost again;
And Joey and me and Wully Scott,
We agreed to ourselves we'd as lief as not
Ha' been found in the thick o' the slain.

By Downpatrick gaol I was bound to fare
On a day I'll remember, feth;
For when I came to the prison square
The people were waitin' in hundreds there,
An' you wouldn't hear stir nor breath!
For the sodgers were standing, grim an' tall,
Round a scaffold built there fornenst the wall,
An' a man stepped out for death.

I was brave an' near the end of the throng,
Yet I knowed the face again,
An' I knowed the set, an' I knowed the walk
An the sound of his strange up-country talk,
For he spoke out right an' plain.
Then he bowed his head to the swinging rope,
Whiles I said, 'Please God' to his dying hope
And 'Amen' to his dying prayer,
That the WRONG would cease and the RIGHT prevail,
For the man that they hanged at Downpatrick gaol
Was the man from GOD-KNOWS-WHERE!

Florence M. Wilson

3

THE BALLAD
OF
WILLIAM BLOAT

In a mean abode on the Shankill Road
   Lived a man called William Bloat.
He had a wife, the curse of his life,
   Who continually got his goat.
So one day at dawn, with her nightdress on,
   He cut her bloody throat.

With a razor gash he settled her hash,
   Oh never was crime so quick,
But the steady drip on the pillow slip
   Of her lifeblood made him sick,
And the pool of gore on the bedroom floor
   Grew clotted cold and thick.

And yet he was glad that he'd done what he had,
   When she lay there stiff and still,
But a sudden awe of the angry law
   Struck his soul with an icy chill.
So to finish the fun so well begun,
   He resolved himself to kill.

Then he took the sheet off his wife's cold feet,
   And twisted it into a rope,
And he hanged himself from the pantry shelf.
   'Twas an easy end, let's hope.
In the face of death with his latest breath,
   He solemnly cursed the Pope.

But the strangest turn to the whole concern
   Is only just beginnin'.
He went to Hell but his wife got well,
   And she's still alive and sinnin',
For the razor blade was German made,
   But the sheet was Irish linen.

                    Raymond Calvert

The Lament of the Irish Emigrant

I'm sitting on the stile, Mary,
Where we sat side by side
On a bright May morning long ago
When first you were my bride.

The corn was springing fresh and green
And the lark sang loud and high
And the red was on your lip, Mary
And the love-light in your eye.

The place is little changed, Mary,
The day as bright as then
The lark's loud song is in my ear
And the corn is green again.

But I miss the soft clasp of your hand
And your breath warm on my cheek
And I still keep listening for the words
You never more will speak.

Yours was the brave good heart, Mary
That still kept hoping on,
When the trust in God had left my soul
And my arm's young strength was gone.

There was comfort ever on your lip
And the kind look on your brow
I bless you for that same, Mary
Tho' you can't hear me now.

Helen, Marchioness of Dufferin and Ava

THE STITCHER

What time is that? It's strikin' four.
My God, to think there's two hours more!
The needles go leapin' along the hem,
And my eyes is dizzy wi' watchin' them.
My back aches cruel, as I lean
And feed the cloth to the machine,
And I hate the noise, and I hate the toil,
And the glarin' lights and the stink of oil;
And yet, it's only strikin' four,
Two hours more, two long hours more!

Well, there's another dozen done,
And here's another lot begun,
When these are finished there are more,
My God, its only just struck four!
And all day long, and every day
I'll sit and stitch the same oul way,
And what's the good? I might ha' been
Born just a part o' my machine,
And not a livin' woman at all;
A wooden figure or a doll,
Has just as much o' life as me,
Tied till a bench, and never free.

Monday morning till Saturday,
I sit and stitch my life away,
I work and sleep and draw my pay,
And every hour I'm growing older,
My cheek is paler, my heart is colder,
And what have ever I done or been,
But just a hand at a sewing-machine?
The needles go leaping along the hem,
And my eyes is sore wi' watching them,
Och! Every time they leap and start,
They pierce my heart – they pierce my heart!

Richard Rowley

NOT DONE YET

My nephews an' my nieces, an' my neighbours every one,
They say my day is over, an' I am oul' an' done,
Only fit in a chair to sit, yawnin' in the sun,
Never to take a dander wi'out their leave an' let;
Och, what a commotion, but I've got a notion,
The oul' fella's not done yet.

It's me is hale an' hearty, an' good for the quare time still;
I can ate my mate, an' polish the plate, an' on fair days drink
   my fill.
There's no better ploughman in Mourne nor me,
Ye can search them where ye will,
I can turn a furrow at frosty dawn,
An' work till the horses sweat,
Let them leave me alone, sure the farm's my own,
An' the oul' fella's not done yet.

But it's 'Uncle, sit down in the corner',
An' it's 'Uncle take a doze':
An' it's 'Never bother to rise the day,
Don't ye see how it rains an' blows';
But I'm the man has got a plan, to turn a new pin in their
   nose,
I've been thinkin' hard, an' considerin' long,
An' now my mind is set,
I'll marry a girl o' twenty year, an' raise a son to follow me
   here.

For the OUL' FELLA'S NOT DONE YET.

Richard Rowley

THE EMIGRANT'S LETTER

Dear Danny,
I'm takin' the pen in me hand
To tell you we're just out o' sight o' the land;
　　In the grand Allan liner we're sailin' in style,
　　But we're sailin' away from the Emerald Isle;
And a long sort o' sigh seemed to rise from us all
As the waves hid the last bit of ould Donegal.
　　Och! it's well to be you that is takin' yer tay
　　Where they're cuttin' the corn in Creeshla the day.

I spoke to the captain – he won't turn her round,
And if I swum back I'd be apt to be drowned,
　　So here I must stay – oh! I've no cause to fret,
　　For their dinner was what you might call a banquet.
But though it is 'sumpchus', I'd swop the whole lot,
For the ould wooden spoon and the stirabout pot;
　　And sweet Katty Farrell a-wettin' the tay
　　Where they're cuttin' the corn in Creeshla the day!

If Katey is courted by Patsey or Mick,
Put a word in for me with a lump of a stick,
　　Don't kill Patsey outright, he has no sort of chance,
　　But Mickey's a rogue you might murther at wance;
For Katey might think as the longer she waits
A boy in the hand is worth two in the States:
　　And she'll promise to honour, to love and obey
　　Some robber that's roamin' round Creeshla the day.

There's a woman on board who knows Katey by sight,
So we talked of ould times till they put out the light.
　I'm to meet the good woman tomorra on deck
　And we'll talk about Katey from this to Quebec.
I know I'm no match for her, oh! not the leesht,
Wid her house and two cows and her brother a preesht,
　But the woman declares Katey's heart's on the say,
　While mine's wid the reapers in Creeshla the day.

Good-bye to you Dan, there's no more to be said,
And I think the salt wather's got into me head,
　For it dreeps from me eyes when I call to me mind,
　The friends and the colleen I'm leavin' behind;
Oh, Danny, she'll wait; whin I bid her good-bye,
There was just the laste taste of a tear in her eye,
　And a break in her voice whin she said, 'you might stay,
　But plaze God you'll come back to ould Creeshla some day.'

Percy French

CARMODY'S MARE

There's the saddlin' bell ringing! – the numbers are up,
Oh, man dear! I must see the race for the Cup.
Push up on that plank there! hi! gimme a hand!
Oh, man! this is better than any Grand Stand.
There's high fliers payin' a shillin' – an' two
That hasn't the half, nor the quarter the view.
Hi! Peter! McGinty! Miginty me son
Come up here an' see the big race bein' run.
– Not room for another? Oh, now you be civil
– Come up here me haro! – An' you to the divil!
Look Peter from here you can see the whole Course
– Ay, call up a policeman, call up the whole Force!
There's the bank an' the hurdles an' there's the stone wall.
An' there's the big water jump, best o' them all.
Who am I backin'? Well, now I declare
I've got all me money on Carmody's mare! –
– Last night it was Carmody gave me the tip
– (You'll be over the rail if ye give any 'lip')
– He told me the ring men were at him agin
To pull the bay mare – but he's riding to win
Thirty pounds if he pulled her! – ay, that's what they said
An' let 'Queen o' the May' come and romp in instead,
But he'll not take their money, he means to ride fair,
An' that's why me shirt is on Carmody's mare.

14

There's Carmody! gallopin' down on the bay,
There's Dimpsey, the robber! on 'Queen o' the May',
There's Flynn on 'The Firefly' – Burke on 'Red Fox',
There's Mangan on 'Merry-legs' – see the white socks,
There's Sweeny on 'Swanshot' – There's Major Tom Goff!
He's linin' them up, boys! – Begorra they're off!
Sit down you in front there! well take off that hat,
I'll take off yer head, if ye give any chat!
Where is he, Peter? Well up in the front?
Oh, don't say that's him at the heel o' the hunt!
Ah, sure, I know why he is keepin' her in,
Yer goin' too fast at the bank, Mr Flynn.
Didn't I tell you, that lep is too wide
No sinsible horse, 'ill take that in his stride.
Ah! look at Carmody – Carmody knows
Hop and go lightly an' over he goes!
What's that yer sayin' there? – Heavens above!
Was there ever a race where a man didn't shove?
Fall off an' be hanged to you, little I care,
As long as Ned Carmody sticks to his mare.
Where is he, Peter? – the Hurdles! well done!
Now, see him off like the shot from a gun!
WILL you sit down, there, I must see the race,
Ye want the contints o' me fist in yer face.
Where is he, Peter! Oh! the stone wall,
Ah, Mr Sweeny, you're out of it all.

Don't let her race at it! Keep her in check!
Or ye'll break her two legs an' yer own silly neck!
Ah! look at Carmody, sinsible chap!
Look at him goin' where Flynn made the gap.
What's that yer talkin' of? What's that you say?
The race is a mortal for 'Queen o' the May'!
Oh, bedad! look at her, sailin' away,
Now, Carmody, Carmody, let out the bay,
– Slash at her, slaughter her, into her now,
'Tis the bay mare that's under you, 'tisn't a cow.
Hustle her, bustle her, drive her across,
'Tis the bay mare that's under you, 'tisn't an ass,
Now, for the Water Jump, grip wid yer thighs,
Rise the mare over it – over she flies!
Look at the two o' them into the straight,
Carmody gains on him! isn't he great?
Now, for a touch o' the spur in her flank,
– D'ye think ye've the lease o' this dirty old plank?
WILL ye go home, and take care o' yer twins?
A thousand pounds level, that Carmody wins!
Didn't I tell ye, ye ignorant calf,
Carmody wins by a lingth an' a half,
Didn't I tell it ye, Peter me son,
Carmody wins, an' I got five to one! –
An' now me good people, I'm just goin' down.
Down to the Bookie to get – me Half-crown.

                                        Percy French

16

AN IRISH MOTHER

A wee slip drawin' water,
   Me ould man at the plough,
No grown-up son nor daughter,
   That's the way we're farmin' now.
'No work and little pleasure'
   Was the cry before they wint,
Now they're gettin' both full measure,
   So I ought to be contint.

Great wages men is givin
   In that land beyant the say,
But 'tis lonely – lonely livin'
   Whin the childher is away.

Och, the baby in the cradle,
   Blue eyes and curlin' hair,
God knows I'd give a gra'dle
   To have little Pether there;
No doubt he'd find it funny
   Lyin' here upon me arm,
Him – that's earnin' the good money,
   On a Californy farm.

Six pounds it was or sivin
   He sint last quarter day,
But 'tis lonely – lonely livin'
   Whin the childher is away.

God is good – none betther,
   And the Divil might be worse,
Each month there comes a letther
   Bringing somethin' for the purse.
And me ould man's heart rejoices
   Whin I read they're doin' fine,
But it's oh! to hear their voices,
   And to feel their hands in mine.

To see the cattle drivin'
And the young ones makin' hay,
'Tis a lonely land to live in
Whin the childher is away.

Whin the shadders do be fallin'
On the ould man there an' me,
'Tis hard to keep from callin'
'Come in, childher, to yer tea!'
I can almost hear them comin'
Mary, Kate and little Con, –
Och! but I'm the foolish woman,
Sure they're all grown up an' gone.

That our sins may be forgiven,
An' not wan go asthray,
I doubt I'd stay in Heaven
If them childher was away.

Percy French

ACH, I DUNNO

I'm simply surrounded by lovers
   Since Da made his fortune in land.
They're coming in flocks like the plovers
   To ax for me hand —
There's clerks and policemen and teachers,
   Some sandy, some black as a crow —
Ma says you get used to the creatures
   But, ach, I dunno —

The convent is in a commotion
   To think of me taking a spouse,
And they wonder I hadn't the notion
   Of taking the vows.
'Tis a beautiful life and a quiet,
   And keeps ye from going below,
As a girl I thought I might try it,
   But, ach, I dunno!

I've none but meself to look after,
   An' marriage it fills me with fears,
I think I'd have less of the laughter
   And more of the tears.
I'll not be a slave like me mother,
   With six of us all in a row,
Even one little baby's a bother,
   But, ach, I dunno!

There's a lad that has taken me fancy,
 I know he's a bit of a limb,
And though marriage is terrible chancy,
 I'd – chance it with him.
He's coming to-night – oh – I tingle
 From the top of me head to me toe,
I'll tell him I'd rather live single,
 But, ach, I dunno!

Percy French

WEE HUGHIE

He's gone to school, wee Hughie,
   An' him not four,
Sure I saw the fright was in him
   When he left the door.

But he took a hand o' Denny,
   An' a hand o' Dan,
Wi' Joe's owld coat upon him –
   Och, the poor wee man!

He cut the quarest figure,
   More stout nor thin;
An' trottin' right an' steady
   Wi' his toes turned in.

I watched him to the corner
   O' the big turf stack,
An' the more his feet went forrit,
   Still his head turned back.

He was lookin', would I call him –
   Och, my heart was woe –
Sure it's lost I am without him,
   But he be to go.

I followed to the turnin'
   When they passed it by,
God help him, he was cryin',
   An', maybe, so was I.

                    Elizabeth Shane

Ach No!

'Listen, Mary Ellen,' says Jimmy to me,
  'There's a dance to-morrow night, will you go?'
But I'm shy in a way where the boys are concerned.
  So says I to him, 'Jimmy, Ach no!
    — Ach no!'

'But the tickets are bought,' says Jimmy, says he,
  'I have them in my pocket and so,
You'll have to come now, for you couldn't let me down,'
  But says I to him, 'Jimmy, Ach no!
    — Ach no!'

On the night o' the dance sure he called at the door,
  'Come on,' says he, 'don't be so slow;
All the boys and the girls from the Braid will be there,'
  But says I to him, 'Jimmy, Ach no!
    — Ach no!'

He's a terrible masterful kind of a lad;
  There was nothin' else for it but to go;
When we got there, says Jimmy, 'We'll show them a step,'
  But says I to him, 'Jimmy, Ach no!
    — Ach no!'

But he took me in his arms and he swung me around,
  And boys! did the saxophone blow;
'Lean your head on my shoulder,' says Jimmy to me,
  But I says to him, 'Jimmy, Ach no!
    — Ach no!'

At the end of the night he was leavin' me home,
   The moon in the sky hangin' low;
'Kiss me good-night now,' says Jimmy, says he;
   But says I to him, 'Jimmy, Ach no!'
     – Ach no!'

'Well, goodbye then,' says Jimmy, 'I'm off to the war;
   I'm joining the Army and so,
I be to be off and you'll see me no more,'
   But says I to him, 'Jimmy, Ach no!
     – Ach no!'

He put his arms round me and gave me a hug;
   I felt like he'd never let go,
'Will you ever,' says he, 'marry anybody else?'
   And says I to him, 'Jimmy, Ach no!
     – Ach no!'

John O' The North

SANDY AND ANDY

Sandy and Andy were two boul' boys,
They jumped out o' bed for they thought they heard a noise.
They looked out the window and what did they see
But three black cats that were sittin' on a tree;
There was one had a fiddle and one had a fife
And one had a drum he was beatin' for his life;
He was beatin' on the drum and cryin' out Ho
At a wee white pig that was sittin' down below,
A wee white pig and a big grey goat
And a cow that was dressed in a polisman's coat.
Says Sandy to Andy, 'Did you ever see the like?'
When up came a bulldog ridin' on a bike;
Says Andy to Sandy, 'It would turn you in the head,'
So they shut down the window and went back to bed.

John O' The North

24

THE WEE YELLOW DOG

When I was a lad I had a wee moiley cow
   And a wee yellow dog called Ben;
I suppose in a way I have far more now,
   But I thought I was the quare fellow then.

There never was the like o' thon wee yellow pup,
   For wherever I went he was there;
He'd come every morning to waken me up
   And whatever I had he got his share.

Up among the heather and down along the glen,
   Rolling in the meadow in the hay;
Boys, right enough we had the great times then,
   Him and me together all the day.

The years are going by and my step's getting slow,
   My hand shakes now and my eyes grow dim;
The wee dog is dead, aye long, long ago,
   And I've never had as good a one as him.

When the last trump calls and I step into the dark,
   To wherever an old man goes;
I somehow think there'll be a friendly bark
   And a welcome from a wee wet nose.

John O' The North

ME AN' ME DA

I'm livin' in Drumlister,
    An' I'm gettin' very oul',
I have to wear an Indian bag
    To save me from the coul'.
The deil a man in this town-lan'
    Wos claner reared nor me,
But I'm livin' in Drumlister
    In clabber to the knee.

Me da lived up in Carmin,
    An' kep a sarvint boy;
His second wife wos very sharp,
    He birried her with joy:
Now she was thin, her name was Flynn,
    She come from Cullentra,
An' if me shirt's a clatty shirt
    The man to blame's me da.

Consarnin' weemin, sure it wos
    A constant word of his,
'Keep far away from them that's thin,
    Their temper's aisy riz.'
Well, I knowed two I thought wud do,
    But still I had me fears,
So I kiffled* back an' forrit
    Between the two, for years.

*'To kiffle,' to make a great fuss and do nothing.

26

Wee Margit had no fortune
   But two rosy cheeks wud plaze;
The farm of lan' wos Bridget's,
   But she tuk the pock disayse:
An' Margit she wos very wee,
   An' Bridget she wos stout,
But her face wos like a Jail dure
   With the bowlts pulled out.

I'll tell no lie on Margit,
   She thought the worl' of me;
I'll tell the thruth me heart wud lep
   The sight of her to see.
But I wos slow, you surely know
   The raisin of it now,
If I left her home from Carmin
   Me da wud rise a row.

So I swithered back an' forrit
   Till Margit got a man;
A fella come from Mullaslin
   An' left me jist the wan.
I mind the day she went away,
   I hid wan strucken hour,
An' cursed the wasp from Cullentra
   That made me da so sour.

But cryin' cures no trouble,
   To Bridget I went back,
An' faced her for it that night week
   Beside her own thurf-stack.
I axed her there, an' spoke her fair
   The handy wife she'd make me,
I talked about the lan' that joined
   — Begob, she wudn't take me!

So I'm livin' in Drumlister,
   An' I'm gettin' very oul',
I creep to Carmin wanst a month
   To thry an' make me sowl:
The deil a man in this town-lan'
   Wos claner reared nor me,
An' I'm dyin' in Drumlister
   In clabber to the knee.

W.F. Marshall

SARAH ANN

I'll change me way of goin', for me head is gettin' grey,
I'm tormented washin' dishes, an' makin' dhraps o' tay;
The kitchen's like a midden, an' the parlour's like a sty,
There's half a fut of clabber on the street outby:
I'll go down agane the morra on me kailey to the Cross
For I'll hif to get a wumman, or the place'll go to loss.

I've fothered all the kettle, an' there's nothin' afther that
But clockin' roun' the ashes wi' an oul Tom cat;
Me very ears is bizzin' from the time I light the lamp,
An' the place is like a graveyard, bar the mare wud give a
    stamp,
So often I be thinkin' an' conthrivin' for a plan
Of how to make the match agane with Robert's Sarah Ann.

I used to make wee Robert's of a Sunday afther prayers,
– Sarah Ann wud fetch the taypot to the parlour up the
    stairs;
An' wance a week for sartin I'd be chappin' at the dure,
There wosn't wan wud open it but her, ye may be sure;
An' then – for all wos goin' well – I got a neighbour man
An' tuk him down to spake for me, an' ax for Sarah Ann.

Did ye iver know wee Robert? Well, he's nothin' but a wart,
A nearbegone oul' divil with a wee black heart,
A crooked, crabbit crathur that bees neither well nor sick,
Girnin' in the chimley corner, or goan happin' on a stick;
Sure ye min' the girl for hirin' that went shoutin' thro' the
      fair,
'I wunthered in wee Robert's, I can summer anywhere.'

But all the same wee Robert has a shap an' farm o' lan',
Ye'd think he'd do it dacent when it come to Sarah Ann;
She bid me ax a hundther'd, an' we worked him up an'
      down,
The deil a hate he'd give her but a cow an' twenty poun';
I pushed for twenty more forbye to help to build a byre,
But ye might as well be talkin' to the stone behin' the fire.

So says I till John, me neighbour, 'Sure we're only lossin'
      time,
Jist let him keep his mollye, I can do without her prime,
Jist let him keep his daughter, the hungry-lukin' nur,
There's jist as chancy weemin, in the countryside as her.'
Man, he let a big thravalley, an' he sent us both – ye know,
But Sarah busted cryin', for she seen we maned till go.

Ay she fell till the cryin', for ye know she isn't young,
She's nearly past her market, but she's civil with her tongue.
That's half a year or thereaways, an' here I'm sittin' yit,
I'll change me way of goin', ay I'll do it while I'm fit,
She a snug well-doin' wumman, no betther in Tyrone,
An' down I'll go the morra, for I'm far too long me lone.

The night the win' is risin', an' it's comin' on to sleet,
It's spittin' down the chimley on the greeshig at me feet,
It's whisslin' at the windy, an' it's roarin' roun' the barn,
There'll be piles of snow the morra on more than
    Mullagharn;
But I'm for tacklin' Sarah Ann; no matter if the snow
Is iverywhere shebowin'; when the morra comes I'll go.

W.F. Marshall

THE NEW MACHINERY

An Inspector came unto my farm
   To view me stock and all I had,
'I'm working for the Board' – says he
   'Your methods here are very bad.
Those nettles should be all cropped up
   And left to ripen in the rain
And every pig should have a cup
   Of cocoa and a currant bun.'

'Your hens' – says he – 'should be fed on glue
   A splendid way to make them sit,
Your goslings should have gaiters too
   To keep their ankles from being wet.
Your milking cows – I'm very sure
   Are not being treated right' – said he
'Your yield of milk is very poor
   Compared with what it ought to be.'

'Have you got music while you milk
   To soothe the old cows' mammary glands?'
I answered – 'No – unless the maid
   Be singing while the milk is canned.'
Well – he heard my answer with a frown
   Then speaking in an angry tone said –
'Go at once into the town
   And buy your cows a gramophone.'

'And every evening in the field
    Play them Beethoven's Overture,
Within a week the extra yield
    Will cover your expenditure.'
He lit his pipe and went away
    To gladden other people's hearts
And I went off and bought this machine of song
    To soothe the old cows' milking parts.

But devil a tune that I could play
    Upon that up-to-date machine
Had any effect – until one day
    I played 'The Wearing Of The Green'.
The Kerry cow threw up her head,
    Kilkenny's tail began to wave,
The Galway cow kicked up her heels
    And each an extra gallon gave.

(*Pause*)

But one old cow from Portadown
    And two that came from near Lough Gall,
Be Jasus – they threw down their heads
    And devil a drop they'd give at all.
And in the end I had to stop
    And drive those other cows away
But still they would not give a drop
    Until I played them 'Dolly's Brae'.

And now I'm in the Devil's fix
   For the blood is up in them old cows
Always arguing politics
   And always breaking into rows.
They won't stand there and eat the grass
   And thus improve their constitutions,
Instead they spend the live-long day
   Passing counter-resolutions.

And dirty chats and running fights
   And disturbing the peace in every way
And when milking time comes round at night
   Sure all I get is curds and whey.

from the *Farmer's Journal*

"HIS MASTER'S VOICE"

The Hottest Wee Widow in Larne

I am a wee widow, I'm near sixty five,
Like a cow I am chewing the cud;
Oh I feel so weary, so fed up, and sad,
Sure I haven't had a coort since the flood;
I married a farmer, he knocked me about,
Till I buried him on his own farm;
And now I'm the hottest wee widow there is,
The hottest wee widow in Larne.

Chorus
    In Whitehead, in Carrick, Kilroot and Raloo,
    In Magheramorne, Glynn and the Barn;
    O, where'er you go, you will find none to bate,
    The hottest wee widow in Larne;
    My boys,
    The hottest wee widow in Larne.

I'll marry another if I get a chance,
For I am a merry oul sport;
And though I am not quite as young as I was,
There's no one dare say I can't court;
If my next man is bashful or simple or shy
I'll soon show him what he's to learn
Oh he'll get a handful whoever gets me,
The hottest wee widow in Larne.

    Chorus

At the wee linen factory on Waterloo Road,
I dung out the office each day;
And I am the sweetheart of all the ould men,
Who empty the boats at the quay;
At Knockemdown's pub on a Saturday night,
I am brimming with Guinness and charm;
The young cubs all say I am with it, you know,
The hottest wee widow in Larne.

Chorus

Louis Gilbert

Sing a Song of York Street

Sing a song of York Street, take me back again
To Big Davey and Buck Alec as they brawl in Stable Lane;
With doffers screamin' round 'em, they fought a brutal bout
Wearin' only trousers, with their bellies hangin' out.

Tell me 'bout the chancers, the hard-chaws and the brass;
Sing a song about the days that all too soon have passed.
The square setts and the pavers and the gas lamps have all
    gone;
The characters have vanished, but the memories linger on.

Tell me 'bout the pawnshops, where yis went when times
    were bleak
And pledged the oul' lad's Sunday suit to see yis through the
    week.
Tell me more of Rinty, an' how he won his crown
On that night yis lit a 'boney' that was seen all over town.

Heagan's home-baked sodas; Wilson's boiled pigs' feet;
Barnie Conway's Guinness; Fenton's finest meat;
Buttermilk from Turner's; Geordie's fresh ice-cream;
The Queen's and Joe McKibben's – all have vanished like a
    dream.

Sometimes I go down there an' sorta make the rounds.
I see them in my mind's eye, and hear their phantom sounds;
I hear the tumblers clinking, and see the faces plain.
Please sing a song of York Street and take me back again.

John Campbell

'CASUAL' CURSES

Did you ever sign on the bloody 'buroo',
   the bloody 'buroo', the bloody 'buroo',
You stand for hours in a big long queue. . .
   In the bloody 'buroo' in Belfast. . .
Did you ever sign on the 'Casual Box',
   the 'Casual Box', the 'Casual Box',
They say them lads take some sad knocks. . .
   On the Casual Box in Belfast. . .
They make you sign there every day,
   every day, every day,
And stop your dole if you go astray. . .
   On the Casual Box in Belfast. . .
Report for work at 8 o'clock, 8 o'clock, 8 o'clock
   but there's no bloody work on the Belfast Dock,
For the Casual man in Belfast. . .
They'll starve yer kids on the word of a jerk,
   word of a jerk, word of a jerk.
Who'll swear ya didn't turn out for work.
   On the Casual Box in Belfast. . .
The way they look when they pay out your dockets,
   pay out your dockets, pay out your dockets.
You'd think it was out of their own bloody pockets,
   In the bloody 'buroo' in Belfast. . .
I hope to God when my life is thru,
   life is thru, life is thru.
Where I go they won't have any bloody 'buroo'. . .
   Like the bloody 'buroo' in Belfast.

                John Campbell

CLOGHER VALLEY RAILWAY

They tuk our oul railway away, so they did,
And sowl the whole lot for a few thousand quid.
They say the ratepayers here are well rid –
Ach, ahmdambut boys, it's tarrah!

For fifty long years she puffed to and fro,
At times she'd get there; at other times no;
She's worth more dead than alive, so must go –
Ach, ahmdambut boys, it's tarrah!

She ran down back gardens and up the Main street
And frightened the horses she happen to meet,
And now she's tuk aff for to build up the fleet –
Ach, ahmdambut boys, it's tarrah!

I hear they're for sellin' the oul line for scrap
For to make into bombs for to plaster the map,
Well, here's hopin' oul Hitler's below when they drap –
Ach, ahmdambut boys, it's tarrah!

They say that the Air Force soon will begin
To use up our Railway, this war for to win;
They'll drap Clogher Station all over Berlin!
Ach, ahmdambut boys, it's tarrah!

Them Nazis now boast of a new submarine,
They say it's the finest that ever was seen;
A CVR depth charge will leave it 'has been' –
Ach, ahmdambut boys, it's tarrah!

When the Roosians and us march down Wilhelmstrasse
Oul Hitler'll say: 'Boys, but I'm the quare ass –
Sure I might have knowed Clogher could still houl the pass.
Ich dambut boys – it's tarrah!'

E.O. Byrne

THE SONG OF THE UNEMPLOYED

We built you graceful structures from a heap of clay and
    stone,
We fashioned out of nothing yonder proud and stately
    dome;
The steeples rising skywards bear the hallmark of our skill,
And the hands that shaped your mansions have the cunning
    in them still.

We levelled fields and ditches to the city's outward stride,
And now you boast its greatness yet we do not share your
    pride;
Our picks have ranged the hillside and our shovels
    smoothed the plain;
That your children might have shelter, though your good
    was not our gain.

You flattered us in labour when our labour brought its due;
The fruits of all our sweat and toil we shared alike with you;
But now our hands lie idle and our hearts are sore with grief,
Comes the clamour of your curses – whilst your praises
    grow more brief.

Thomas Carnduff

40

Cover design for 1932 Quota Press collection of Carnduff's poems.

Seaġan. maċċaṫmaoil· del.

HERSELF COME BACK

All the folk in our hoose
    Shure they think I'm quare
For sittin' at nights
    In my ould armchair;
An' niver goin' oot,
    At the set o' sun,
For a breath o' air
    When the work's all done.

But, ah! if they knowed
    Jist why I stay in,
They'd all o' them think it
    A mortyil sin,
For tae deeve my head
    Wi' their addle-talk,
An' quit their coaxin'
    Me oot a walk.

But how cud they know
　　When I've niver toul'
The raison o' it
　　Tae a single sowl?
Thank God. They're gone oot.
　　Now, beside the fire,
I'll can see an' spake
　　Till my Heart's Desire.

When she comes I'll loosen
　　Her hair's black bands,
I'll whisper her name,
　　An' I houl' her hands,
An' I'll kiss her eyes –
　　Yes o' mild blue-grey –
As I did, while she died,
　　That May Saturday.

An' she'll lie a wee while
　　On my heart again:
An' I'll know white peace,
　　An' I'll know red pain;
An' the loneliness
　　That I bear all day,
As she smoothes my hair,
　　Will all pass away.

Wheest! Wheest! There's her step!
　　Wheest! She's comin' in.
She can come wi'oot
　　Tirlin' the latch's pin.
Oh, come in, my wife,
　　Oh, come in, my own,
I'm waitin' in here,
　　In the gloom, m'lone.

Padraig Gregory

43

The Three Stages

When Lizzie Grahame wus near eighteen,
  She had the quare proud air;
An' all the bhoys wud follow her
  Thro' Ballymena Fair,
    (*They wud!*)
  Thro' Ballymena Fair.
But if a lad dar'd smile, she'd toss
  Her head so brown an' frizzy,
An' tilt her nose, an' ax out loud,
  Behint hes back, '*Who* is he?'

When Lizzie Grahame 'd turned twenty-eight,
  She'd got a titterin' air;
An' only some looked afther her
  At Ballymena Fair,
    (*Jist some!*)
  At Ballymena Fair.
An' when an odd wan spoke she'd stan',
  Cologuin' long, wud Lizzie;
An', thinkin' only o' a match,
  She'd ax some friend: '*What* is he?'

Now, Lizzie Grahame's near thirty-eight,
  An' has a could peeked air;
An' divil a body bothers her
  In Ballymena Fair,
    (*Not wan!*)
  In Ballymena Fair.
But, last week, when some strange sowl smiled,
  Surprise near knocked her dizzy,
But soon she had the whole Fair up
  Wi' yellin' out: '*Where* is he?'

Padraig Gregory

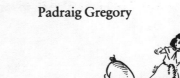

THE DIAGONAL STEAM-TRAP

Now they built a big ship down in Harland's –
She was made for to sell till the Turks –
And they called on the Yard's chief designer
To design all the engines and works.

Now finally the engines was ready
And they screwed in the very last part
An' yer man says 'Let's see how she runs, lads!'
An' bejasus! the thing wouldn't start!

So they pushed and they worked an' they footered
An' the engineers' faces got red
The designer he stood lookin' stupid
An' scratchin' the back o' his head.

But while they were fiddlin' and workin'
Up danders oul' Jimmie Dalzell
He had worked twenty years in the 'Island'
And ten in the 'aircraft' as well.

So he pushed and he worked and he muttered
Till he got himself through till the front
And he has a good look roun' the engine
An' he gives a few mutters and grunts,

And then he looks up at the gaffer
An' says he 'Mr Smith, d'ye know?
They've left out the Diagonal Steam Trap!
How the hell d'ye think it could go?'

Now the engineer eyed the designer
The designer he looks at the 'hat'
And they whispered the one to the other
'Diagonal Steam Trap? What's that?'

But the Gaffer, he wouldn't admit, like
To not knowin' what this was about,
So he says 'Right enough, we were stupid!
The Diagonal Steam Trap's left out!'

Now in the meantime oul' Jimmie had scarpered
– away down to throw in his boord –
And the Gaffer comes up and says 'Jimmy!
D'ye think we could have a wee word?'

Ye see that Diagonal Steam Trap?
I know it's left out – it's bad luck
But the engine shop's terrible busy
D'ye think ye could knock us one up?'

Now, oul' Jimmy was laughin' his scone off
He had made it all up for a gag
He seen what was stoppin' the engine –
The feed-pipe was blocked with a rag!

But he sticks the oul' hands in the pockets
An' he says 'Aye, I'll give yez a han'!
I'll knock yes one up in the mornin'
An' the whole bloody thing will be grand!'

So oul' Jim starts to work the next morning
To make what he called a Steam Trap,
An oul' box an' a few bits of tubing
An' a steam gauge stuck up on the top,

An' he welds it all on till the engine
And he says to the wonderin' mob
'As long as that gauge is at zero
The Steam Trap is doin' its job!'

Then he pulls the rag outa the feed pipe
An' he gives the oul' engine a try
An' bejasus! she goes like the clappers
An' oul' Jimmy remarks 'That's her nye!'

Now the ship was the fastest seen ever
So they sent her away till the Turks
But they toul' them 'That Steam Trap's a secret!
We're the only ones knows how it works!'

But the Turks they could not keep their mouths shut
An' soon the whole story got roun'
An' the Russians got quite interested –
– Them boys has their ears till the groun'!

So they sent a spy dressed as a sailor
To take photies of Jimmy's Steam Trap
And they got them all back till the Kremlin
An' they stood round to look at the snaps.

Then the head spy says 'Mr Kosygin!
I'm damned if I see how that works!'
So they sent him straight off to Siberia
An' they bought the whole ship from the Turks!

When they found the Steam Trap was a 'cod', like,
They couldn't admit they'd been had
So they built a big factory in Moscow
To start makin' Steam Traps like mad!

Then Kosygin rings up Mr Nixon
And he says 'Youse'uns thinks yez are great!
But wi' our big new Russian-made Steam Trap
Yez'll find that we've got yez all bate!'

Now oul Nixon, he nearly went 'harpic'
So he thought he'd give Harland's a call
And he dialled the engine-shop number
And of course he got sweet bugger all!

But at last the call came through to Jimmy
In the midst of a terrible hush,
'There's a call for you here from the White House!'
Says oul' Jim, 'That's a shop in Portrush!'

There's a factory outside of Seattle
Where they're turnin' out Steam Traps like Hell
It employs twenty-five thousand workers
And the head of it – Jimmy Dalzell!

Crawford Howard

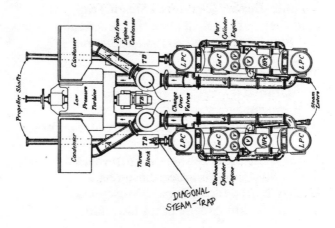

WHEN I WAS A LITTLE GIRL

WHEN I was a little girl,
  In a garden playing
A thing was often said
To chide us delaying:

When after sunny hours,
At twilight's falling,
Down through the garden walks
Came our old nurse calling,

'Come in! for it's growing late,
And the grass will wet ye!
Come in! or when it's dark
The Fenians will get ye.'

Then, at this dreadful news,
All helter-skelter,
The panic-struck little flock
Ran home for shelter.

And round the nursery fire
Sat still to listen,
Fifty bare toes on the hearth,
Ten eyes a-glisten.

To hear of a night in March,
And loyal folk waiting,
To see a great army of men
Come devastating.

An Army of Papists grim,
With a green flag o'er them,
Red-coats and black police
Flying before them.

But God (Who our nurse declared
Guards British dominions)
Sent down a fall of snow
And scattered the Fenians.

'But somewhere they're lurking yet,
Maybe they're near us,'
Four little hearts pit-a-pat
Thought 'Can they hear us?'

Then the wind-shaken pane
Sounded like drumming;
'Oh!' they cried, 'tuck us in,
The Fenians are coming!'

Four little pairs of hands
In the cots where she led those,
Over their frightened heads
Pulled up the bedclothes.

But one little rebel there,
Watching all with laughter,
Thought, 'When the Fenians come
I'll rise and go after.'

Wished she had been a boy
And a good deal older –
Able to walk for miles
With a gun on her shoulder.

Able to lift aloft
The Green Flag o'er them
(Red-coats and black police
Flying before them).

And, as she dropped asleep,
Was wondering whether
God, if they prayed to Him,
Would give fine weather.

                              Alice Milligan

AN OLD WOMAN OF THE ROADS

Seajan·mac Cat maoil·del.

Oh, to have a little house!
   To own the hearth and stool and all!
The heaped-up sods upon the fire,
   The pile of turf against the wall!

To have a clock with weights and chains
   And pendulum swinging up and down!
A dresser filled with shining delph,
   Speckled and white and blue and brown!

I could be busy all the day
   Clearing and sweeping hearth and floor,
And fixing on their shelf again
   My white and blue and speckled store!

I could be quiet there at night
   Beside the fire and by myself,
Sure of a bed, and loth to leave
   The ticking clock and the shining delph!

Och! but I'm weary of mist and dark,
   And roads where there's never a house or bush,
And tired I am of bog and road
   And the crying wind and the lonesome hush!

And I am praying to God on high,
   And I am praying Him night and day,
For a little house — a house of my own —
   Out of the wind's and the rain's way.

                       Padraic Colum

Seaȝan · mac Carmaoil · del.

THE BALLAD OF MASTER M'GRATH

Eighteen-Sixty-Eight being the state of the year,
Them Waterloo sportsmen did grandly appear
To gain the great prizes and bear them awa',
Never countin' on Ireland and Master M'Gra'.

On the 12th of December, that day of renown,
M'Gra' and his trainer they left Lurgan Town;
John Walsh was the trainer, and soon they got o'er,
For the very next day they touched England's sweet shore.

And when they arrived there in great London Town,
All the fine English sportsmen they gathered aroun'.
An' one of the gentlemen gave a 'Ha! Ha!'
Sayin': 'Is that the great dog you call Master M'Gra'?'

Then Lord Lurgan steps forward and says: 'Gentlemen,
If there's any among you has money to spen',
For youse nobles of England I don't care a straw,
Here's five thousand to one on my Master M'Gra'.'

Then M'Gra' he looked up and he wagged his oul' tail
Just to comfort his Lordship and show he'd not fail,
While Rose stood uncovered and the crowd yelled 'Hurrah,
There's the pride of all England and Master M'Gra'.'

As Rose and the Master both waited their call,
'Now I wonder,' said Rose, 'why you left home at all.'
'Keep your breath for the race and don't waste it on jaw,
And snuff that up your neb,' said oul' Master M'Gra'.

The hare she went off just as swift as the wind,
He was sometimes fornenst her and sometimes behind
Rose gave the first turn, all accordin' to law,
But the second was given by Master M'Gra'.

Then the hare she led on with a beautiful view,
An' swift as the wind o'er the green fields she flew,
But he jumped on her back and held up his oul' paw,
And 'Three cheers for oul' Irelan',' cried Master M'Gra'.

Anon.

55

THE FLOWER OF SWEET STRABANE

If I were King of Ireland,
  And all things at my will,
I'd roam through recreation
  New comforts to find still;
And the comfort I would seek the most,
  You all may understand,
Is to win the hand of Martha –
  She's the Flow'r of Sweet Strabane.

Her cheeks they are rosy red,
  And her eyes a lovely brown,
And over her lily-white shoulders
  Her hair of brown hangs down;
She is one of the fairest creatures,
  And famous in her clan,
And my heart is captivated
  With the Flower of Sweet Strabane.

If I had you, lovely Martha,
  Away in Inishowen,
Or in some lonely valley
  In the wild woods of Tyrone,
I would use my whole endeavour,
  And try to work my plan
For to gain my prize and feast my eyes
  On the Flower of Sweet Strabane.

But farewell to bonny Lifford,
  Where the Sweet Mourne waters flow,
And likewise unto my brown-haired girl,
  Since I from her must go;
As down Lough Foyle the waters boil,
  And my ship it stands out from land,
I will say farewell and God bless you
  To my Flower of Sweet Strabane.

Traditional

The
Ould Orange Flute

In the County Tyrone, near the town of Dungannon,
  Where many's the ruction myself had a han' in,
Bob Williamson lived, a weaver by trade,
  And all of us thought him a stout Orange blade.
On the Twelfth of July, as it yearly did come,
  Bob played on the flute to the sound of the drum.
You may talk of your harp, your piano, or lute,
  But nothing could sound like the ould Orange flute.

But Bob the deceyver, he took us all in,
  For he married a Papish called Bridget McGinn,
Turned Papish himself, and forsook the ould cause
  That gave us our freedom, religion and laws.
Now, the boys in the townland made comment upon it,
  And Bob had to fly to the province of Connaught.
He flew with his wife, and his fixin's to boot,
  And along with the others the ould Orange flute.

At the Chapel on Sundays to atone for past deeds,
  He said 'Paters' and 'Aves' and counted his beads,
Till, after some time, at the priest's own desire,
  He went with his ould flute to play in the choir,
He went with his ould flute to play in the Mass,
  But the instrument shivered and sighed, Oh alas!
When he blew it and fingered and made a great noise,
  The flute would play only 'The Protestant Boys'.

Bob jumped and he started and got in a splutter,
  And threw the ould flute in the Bless'd Holy Water;
He thought that this charm might bring some other sound.
  When he blew it again, it played 'Croppies Lie Down',
And all he could whistle and finger and blow,
  To play Papish music he found it no go.
'Kick the Pope', 'The Boyne Water' and such like it would sound,
  But one Papish squeak in it couldn't be found.

At a council of priests that was held the next day,
  They decided to banish the ould flute away;
For they couldn't knock heresy out of its head,
  And they bought Bob another to play in its stead.
So the ould flute was doomed and its fate was pathetic;
  It was fastened and burned at the stake as a heretic.
While the flames roared around it, they heard a strange noise –
  'Twas the ould flute still whistlin' 'The Protestant Boys'!

Traditional

59

LET THE TOAST PASS

Here's to the maiden of bashful fifteen,
   Here's to the widow of fifty;
Here's to the flaunting extravagant queen,
   And here's to the housewife that's thrifty.

Chorus

   Let the toast pass,
   Drink to the lass,
I'll warrant she'll prove an excuse for the glass.

Here's to the charmer whose dimples we prize,
   Now to the maid who has none, sir,
Here's to the girl with a pair of blue eyes,
   And here's to the nymph with but one, sir!

   Let the toast pass, etc.

Here's to the maid with a bosom of snow,
   And to her that's as brown as a berry;
Here's to the wife, with a face full of woe,
   And now to the damsel that's merry:

   Let the toast pass, etc.

For let 'em be clumsy, or let 'em be slim,
   Young or ancient, I care not a feather;
So fill the pint bumper quite up to the brim,
   And let us e'en toast them together:

Chorus

   Let the toast pass,
   Drink to the lass,
I'll warrant she'll prove an excuse for the glass.

Richard Brinsley Sheridan

A GLASS OF BEER

The lanky hank of a she in the inn over there
Nearly killed me for asking the loan of a glass of beer;
May the devil grip the whey-faced slut by the hair,
And beat bad manners out of her skin for a year.

That parboiled ape, with the toughest jaw you will see
On virtue's path, and a voice that would rasp the dead,
Came roaring and raging the minute she looked at me,
And threw me out of the house on the back of my head!

If I asked her master he'd give me a cask a day;
But she, with the beer at hand, not a gill would arrange!
May she marry a ghost and bear him a kitten, and may
The High King of Glory permit her to get the mange.

James Stephens

61

JOHNNY McELDOO

There was Johnny McEldoo and McGee and me
And a couple or two or three went on a spree one day.
We had a bob or two which we knew how to blew
And the beer and whiskey flew and we all felt gay.
We visited McCann's, McIllmann's, Humpty Dan's,
We then went into Swann's our stomachs for to pack.
We ordered out a feed which indeed we did need
And we finished it with speed but we still felt slack.

Johnny McEldoo turned red, white and blue
When a plate of Irish stew he soon put out of sight,
He shouted out 'Encore' with a roar for some more
That he never felt before such a keen appetite.
He ordered eggs and ham, bread and jam, what a cram!
But him we couldn't ram though we tried our level best,
For everything we brought, cold or hot, mattered not,
It went down him like a shot, but he still stood the test.

He swallowed tripe and lard by the yard, we got scared,
We thought it would go hard when the waiter brought the
    bill.
We told him to give o'er, but he swore he could lower
Twice as much again and more before he had his fill.
He nearly supped a trough full of broth. Says McGrath,
'He'll devour the tablecloth if you don't hold him in.'
When the waiter brought the charge, McEldoo felt so large
He began to scowl and barge and his blood went on fire.

He began to curse and swear, tear his hair in despair,
And to finish the affair called the shopman a liar.
The shopman he drew out, and no doubt, he did clout
McEldoo he kicked about like an old football
He tattered all his clothes, broke his nose, I suppose
He'd have killed him with a few blows in no time at all.

McEldoo began to howl and to growl, by my sowl
He threw an empty bowl at the shopkeepers head.
It struck poor Mickey Flynn, peeled the skin off his chin
And the ructions did begin and we all fought and bled.
The peelers did arrive, man alive, four or five,
At us they made a drive for us all to march away.
We paid for all the mate, that we ate, stood a trate,
And went home to reminate on the spree that day.

Anon.

Johnny Sands

A man whose name was Johnny Sands
Had married Betty Haig
Though she brought him gold and land
She proved a terrible plague.

Says he 'I will drown myself
The river runs below.'
Says she 'pray do, you silly elf
I wished it long ago.'

'For fear that I should courage lack
And try to save my life
Pray tie my hands behind my back.'
'I will,' replied his wife.

All down the hill his loving bride
Now ran with all her force,
To push him in, he stepped aside
And she fell in, of course.

Now splashing, dashing like a fish
'O save me Johnny Sands.'
'I can't my dear, though much I wish
For you have tied my hands.'

Anon.

BALLAD TO A TRADITIONAL REFRAIN

Red brick in the suburbs, white horse on the wall,
Eyetalian marble in the City Hall:
O stranger from England, why stand so aghast?
May the Lord in His mercy be kind to Belfast.

This jewel that houses our hopes and our fears
Was knocked up from the swamp in that last hundred years;
But the last shall be first and the first shall be last;
May the Lord in His mercy be kind to Belfast.

We swore by King William there'd never be seen
An All-Irish Parliament at College Green,
So at Stormont we're nailing the flag to the mast:
May the Lord in His mercy be kind to Belfast.

O the bricks they will bleed and the rain it will weep,
And the damp Lagan fog lull the city to sleep;
It's to hell with the future and live on the past:
May the Lord in His mercy be kind to Belfast.

Maurice James Craig

65

Favourite
Imports

THE CREMATION OF SAM McGEE

There are strange things done in the midnight sun
  By the men who moil for gold;
The Arctic trails have their secret tales
  That would make your blood run cold;
The Northern Lights have seen queer sights,
  But the queerest they ever did see
Was that night on the marge of Lake Lebarge
  I cremated Sam McGee.

Now Sam McGee was from Tennessee, where the
  cotton blooms and blows.
Why he left his home in the South to roam round
  the Pole God only knows.
He was always cold, but the land of gold seemed
  to hold him like a spell;
Though he'd often say in his homely way that
  he'd 'sooner live in hell'.

On a Christmas Day we were mushing our way
  over the Dawson trail.
Talk of your cold! through the parka's fold it
  stabbed like a driven nail.
If our eyes we'd close, then the lashes froze, till
  sometimes we couldn't see;
It wasn't much fun, but the only one to whimper
  was Sam McGee.

And that very night as we lay packed tight in our
  robes beneath the snow,
And the dogs were fed, and the stars o'erhead
  were dancing heel and toe,
He turned to me, and, 'Cap,' says he, 'I'll cash
  in this trip, I guess;
And if I do, I'm asking that you won't refuse my
  last request.'

Well, he seemed so low that I couldn't say no:
    then he says with a sort of moan:
'It's the cursèd cold, and it's got right hold till
    I'm chilled clean through to the bone.
Yet 'taint being dead, it's my awful dread of the
    icy grave that pains:
So I want you to swear that, foul or fair, you'll
    cremate my last remains.'

A pal's last need is a thing to heed, so I swore I
    would not fail;
And we started on at the streak of dawn, but God!
    he looked ghastly pale.
He crouched on the sleigh, and he raved all day
    of his home in Tennessee;
And before nightfall a corpse was all that was left
    of Sam McGee.

There wasn't a breath in that land of death, and
    I hurried, horror driven,
With a corpse half-hid that I couldn't get rid
    because of a promise given;
It was lashed to the sleigh, and it seemed to say:
    'You may tax your brawn and brains,
But you promised true, and it's up to you to
    cremate those last remains.'

Now a promise made is a debt unpaid, and the
    trail has its own stern code.
In the days to come, though my lips were dumb,
    in my heart how I cursed that load.
In the long, long night, by the lone firelight, while
    the huskies, round in a ring,
Howled out their woes to the homeless snows – O
    God! how I loathed the thing!

And every day that quiet clay seemed to heavy
    and heavier grow;
And on I went, though the dogs were spent and
    the grub was getting low;
The trail was bad, and I felt half mad, but I swore
    I would not give in;
And I'd often sing to the hateful thing, and it
    hearkened with a grin.

Till I came to the marge of Lake Lebarge, and a
    derelict there lay;
It was jammed in the ice, but I saw in a trice it
    was called the 'Alice May'.
And I looked at it, and I thought a bit, and I
    looked at my frozen chum:
Then, 'Here,' said I, with a sudden cry, 'is my
    cre-ma-tor-eum.'

Some planks I tore from the cabin floor, and I lit
    the boiler fire;
Some coal I found that was lying around, and I
    heaped the fuel higher;
The flames just soared, and the furnace roared –
    such a blaze you seldom see;
And I burrowed a hole in the glowing coal, and I
    stuffed in Sam McGee.

Then I made a hike, for I didn't like to hear him
    sizzle so;
And the heavens scowled, and the huskies howled,
    and the wind began to blow.
It was icy cold, but the hot sweat rolled down my
    cheeks, and I don't know why;
And the greasy smoke in an inky cloak went
    streaking down the sky.

I do not know how long in the snow I wrestled
    with grisly fear;
But the stars came out and they danced about ere
    again I ventured near;
I was sick with dread, but I bravely said: 'I'll
    just take a peep inside.
I guess he's cooked, and it's time I looked,'
    then the door I opened wide.

And there sat Sam, looking cool and calm, in the
    heart of the furnace roar;
And he wore a smile you could see a mile, and he
    said: 'Please close that door.
It's fine in here, but I greatly fear you'll let in the
    cold and storm —
Since I left Plumtree, down in Tennessee, it's the
    first time I've been warm.'

There are strange things done in the midnight sun
    By the men who moil for gold;
The Arctic trails have their secret tales
    That would make your blood run cold
The Northern Lights have seen queer sights,
    But the queerest they ever did see
Was the night on the marge of Lake Lebarge
    I cremated Sam McGee.

Robert Service

THE SHOOTING OF DAN McGREW

A bunch of the boys were whooping it up in the
Malamute saloon;
The kid that handles the music-box was hitting a
jag-time tune;
Back of the bar, in a solo game, sat Dangerous
Dan McGrew,
And watching his luck was his light-o'-love, the
lady that's known as Lou.

When out of the night, which was fifty below,
and into the din and the glare,
There stumbled a miner fresh from the creeks,
dog-dirty and loaded for bear.
He looked like a man with a foot in the grave,
and scarcely the strength of a louse,
Yet he tilted a poke of dust on the bar, and he
called for drinks for the house.
There was none could place the stranger's face,
though we searched ourselves for a clue;
But we drank his health, and the last to drink
was Dangerous Dan McGrew.

There's men that somehow just grip your eyes,
and hold them hard like a spell;
And such was he, and he looked to me like a
man who had lived in hell;
With a face most hair, and the dreary stare of a
dog whose day is done,
As he watered the green stuff in his glass, and
the drops fell one by one.
Then I got to figgering who he was, and wondering
what he'd do,
And I turned my head – and there watching him
was the lady that's known as Lou.

His eyes went rubbering round the room, and he
    seemed in a kind of daze,
Till at last that old piano fell in the way of his
    wandering gaze.
The rag-time kid was having a drink; there was
    no one else on the stool,
So the stranger stumbles across the room, and
    flops down there like a fool.
In a buckskin shirt that was glazed with dirt he
    sat, and I saw him sway;
Then he clutched the keys with his talon hands –
    my God! but that man could play!

Where you ever out in the Great Alone, when the
    moon was awful clear,
And the icy mountains hemmed you in with a
    silence you most could *hear;*
With only the howl of a timber wolf, and you
    camped there in the cold,
A half-dead thing in a stark, dead world, clean
    mad for the muck called gold;
While high overhead, green, yellow, and red, the
    North Lights swept in bars –
Then you've a hunch what the music meant . . .
    hunger and night and the stars.

And hunger not of the belly kind, that's banished
    with bacon and beans;
But the gnawing hunger of lonely men for a home
    and all that it means;
For a fireside far from the cares that are, four
    walls and a roof above;
But oh! so cramful of cosy joy, and crowned
    with a woman's love;
A woman dearer than all the world, and true as
    Heaven is true –
(God! how ghastly she looks through her rouge, –
    that lady that's known as Lou.)

Then on a sudden the music changed, so soft that
    you scarce could hear;
But you felt that your life had been looted clean
    of all that it once held dear;
That some one had stolen the woman you loved;
    that her love was a devil's lie;
That your guts were gone, and the best for you
    was to crawl away and die.
'Twas the crowning cry of a heart's despair, and
    it thrilled you through and through –
'I guess I'll make it a spread misere,' said
    Dangerous Dan McGrew.

The music almost died away. . . then it burst
    like a pent-up flood;
And it seemed to say, 'Repay, repay', and my
    eyes were blind with blood.
The thought came back of an ancient wrong, and
    it stung like a frozen lash,
And the lust awoke to kill, to kill. . . then the
    music stopped with a crash,

And the stranger turned, and his eyes they burned
    in a most peculiar way;
In a buckskin shirt that was glazed with dirt he
    sat, and I saw him sway;
Then his lips went in in a kind of grin, and he
    spoke, and his voice was calm;
And, 'Boys,' says he, 'you don't know me, and
    none of you care a damn;
But I want to state, and my words are straight,
    and I'll bet my poke they're true,
That one of you is a hound of hell. . . and that
    one is Dan McGrew.'

Then I ducked my head, and the lights went out,
    and two guns blazed in the dark;
And a woman screamed, and the lights went up,
    and two men lay stiff and stark;
Pitched on his head, and pumped full of lead, was
    Dangerous Dan McGrew,
While the man from the creeks lay clutched to
    the breast of the lady that's known as Lou.

These are the simple facts of the case, and I guess
    I ought to know;
They say that the stranger was crazed with
    'hooch', and I'm not denying it's so.
I'm not so wise as the lawyer guys, but strictly
    between us two –
The woman that kissed him and – pinched his
    poke – was the lady that's known as Lou.

Robert Service

LITTLE BOY BLUE

THE little toy dog is covered with dust,
   But sturdy and staunch he stands;
   And the little toy soldier is red with rust,
And his musket moulds in his hands.
Time was when the little toy dog was new,
   And the soldier was passing fair;
And that was the time when our Little Boy Blue
   Kissed them and put them there.

'Now, don't you go till I come,' he said,
   'And don't you make any noise!'
So, toddling off to his trundle-bed,
   He dreamt of the pretty toys;
And, as he was dreaming, an angel song
   Awakened our Little Boy Blue –
Oh! the years are many, the years are long,
   But the little toy friends are true!

Ay, faithful to Little Boy Blue they stand,
   Each in the same old place,
Awaiting the touch of a little hand,
   The smile of a little face;
And they wonder, as waiting the long years through
   In the dust of that little chair,
What has become of our Little Boy Blue,
   Since he kissed them and put them there.

                                   Eugene Field

HOHENLINDEN

On Linden when the sun was low,
All bloodless lay the untrodden snow,
And dark as winter was the flow
   Of Iser, rolling rapidly.
But Linden saw another sight
When the drum beat at dead of night,
Commanding fires of death to light
   The darkness of her scenery.

By torch and trumpet fast array'd,
Each horseman drew his battle-blade,
And furious every charger neigh'd
   To join the dreadful revelry.
Then shook the hills with thunder riven,
Then rush'd the steed to battle driven,
And louder than the bolts of heaven
   Far flash'd the red artillery!

But redder yet that light shall glow
On Linden's hills of stainèd snow,
And bloodier yet the torrent flow
   Of Iser, rolling rapidly.
'Tis morn, but scarce yon level sun
Can pierce the war-clouds rolling dun,
When furious Frank and fiery Hun
   Shout in their sulphurous canopy!

The combat deepens, On, ye brave,
Who rush to glory or the grave!
Wave, Munich! all thy banners wave,
   And charge with all thy chivalry.
Few, few shall part where many meet!
The snow shall be their winding-sheet,
And every turf beneath their feet
   Shall be a soldier's sepulchre.

          Thomas Campbell

THE CHARGE OF THE LIGHT BRIGADE

Half a league, half a league,
  Half a league onward,
All in the valley of Death
  Rode the six hundred.
'Forward, the Light Brigade!
Charge for the guns!' he said;
Into the valley of Death
  Rode the six hundred.

'Forward, the Light Brigade!'
Was there a man dismay'd?
Not tho' the soldier knew
  Some one had blunder'd:
Theirs not to make reply,
Theirs not to reason why,
Theirs but to do and die:
Into the valley of Death
  Rode the six hundred.

Cannon to right of them,
Cannon to left of them,
Cannon in front of them
  Volley'd and thunder'd;
Storm'd at with shot and shell,
Boldly they rode and well,
Into the jaws of Death,
Into the mouth of Hell
  Rode the six hundred.

Flash'd all their sabres bare,
Flash'd as they turn'd in air,
Sabring the gunners there,
Charging an army, while
    All the world wonder'd:
Plunged in the battery-smoke
Right thro' the line they broke;
Cossack and Russian
Reel'd from the sabre-stroke
    Shatter'd and sunder'd.
Then they rode back, but not,
    Not the six hundred.

Cannon to right of them,
Cannon to left of them,
Cannon behind them
    Volley'd and thunder'd;
Storm'd at with shot and shell,
While horse and hero fell,
They that had fought so well
Came thro' the jaws of Death
Back from the mouth of Hell,
All that was left of them,
    Left of six hundred.

When can their glory fade?
O the wild charge they made!
    All the world wonder'd.
Honour the charge they made!
Honour the Light Brigade,
    Noble six hundred!

                              Lord Tennyson

CASABIANCA

The boy stood on the burning deck
    Whence all but he had fled;
The flame that lit the battle's wreck
    Shone round him o'er the dead.

The flames rolled on. He would not go
    Without his father's word;
That father faint in death below,
    His voice no longer heard.

He called aloud: 'Say, father, say
    If yet my task is done!'
He knew not that the chieftain lay
    Unconscious of his son.

'Speak, father!' once again he cried,
    'If I may yet be gone!'
And but the booming shots replied,
    And fast the flames rolled on.

Upon his brow he felt their breath,
    And in his waving hair,
And looked from that lone post of death
    In still yet brave despair;

And shouted but once more aloud,
    'My father! must I stay?'
While o'er him fast through sail and shroud,
    The wreathing fires made way.

They wrapt the ship in splendour wild,
    They caught the flag on high,
And streamed above the gallant child
    Like banners in the sky.

Then came a burst of thunder-sound —
    The boy — oh! where was he?
Ask of the winds that far around
    With fragments strewed the sea,

With mast, and helm, and pennon fair,
    That well had borne their part.
But the noblest thing that perished there
    Was that young faithful heart.

Felicia Hemans

GUNGA DIN

You may talk o' gin and beer
When you're quartered safe out 'ere,
An' you're sent to penny fights an' Aldershot it;
But when it comes to slaughter
You will do your work on water,
An' you'll lick the bloomin' boots of 'im that's got it.
Now in Injia's sunny clime,
Where I used to spend my time
A-servin' of 'Er Majesty the Queen,
Of all them blackfaced crew
The finest man I knew
Was our regimental bhisti, Gunga Din.
        He was 'Din! Din! Din!
    'You limpin' lump o' brick-dust, Gunga Din!
        'Hi! slippy *hitherao*!
        'Water, get it! *Panee lao*![1]
    'You squidgy-nosed old idol, Gunga Din.'

The uniform 'e wore
Was nothin' much before,
An' rather less than 'arf o' that be'ind,
For a piece o' twisty rag
An' a goatskin water-bag
Was all the field-equipment 'e could find.
When the sweatin' troop-train lay
In a sidin' through the day,
Where the 'eat would make your bloomin' eyebrows crawl,
We shouted 'Harry By!'[2]
Till our throats were bricky-dry,
Then we wopped 'im 'cause 'e couldn't serve us all.
        It was 'Din! Din! Din!
    'You 'eathen, where the mischief 'ave you been?
        'You put some *juldee*[3] in it
        'Or I'll *marrow*[4] you this minute
    'If you don't fill up my helmet, Gunga Din!'

81

'E would dot an' carry one
Till the longest day was done;
An' 'e didn't seem to know the use o' fear.
If we charged or broke or cut,
You could bet your bloomin' nut,
'E'd be waitin' fifty paces right flank rear.
With 'is mussick⁵ on 'is back,
'E would skip with our attack,
An' watch us till the bugles made 'Retire',
An' for all 'is dirty 'ide
'E was white, clear white, inside
When 'e went to tend the wounded under fire!
    It was 'Din! Din! Din!'
  With the bullets kickin' dust-spots on the green.
    When the cartridges ran out,
    You could hear the front-files shout,
  'Hi, ammunition-mules an' Gunga Din!'

I sha'n't forgit the night
When I dropped be'ind the fight
With a bullet where my belt-plate should 'a' been.
I was chokin' mad with thirst,
An' the man that spied me first
Was our good old grinnin', gruntin' Gunga Din.
'E lifted up my 'ead,
An' he plugged me where I bled,
An' 'e guv me 'arf-a-pint o' water green.
It was crawlin' and it stunk,
But of all the drinks I've drunk,
I'm gratefullest to one from Gunga Din.
    It was 'Din! Din! Din!
    ''Ere's a beggar with a bullet through 'is spleen;
    ''E's chawin' up the ground,
    'An' 'e's kickin' all around:
  'For Gawd's sake git the water, Gunga Din!'

'E carried me away
To where a dooli lay,
An' a bullet come an' drilled the beggar clean.
'E put me safe inside,
An' just before 'e died,
'I 'ope you liked your drink,' sez Gunga Din.
So I'll meet 'im later on
At the place where 'e is gone —
Where it's always double drill and no canteen.
'E 'll be squattin' on the coals
Givin' drink to poor damned souls,
An' I'll get a swig in hell from Gunga Din!
  Yes, Din! Din! Din!
 You Lazarushian-leather Gunga Din!
  Though I've belted you and flayed you,
  By the livin' Gawd that made you,
 You're a better man than I am, Gunga Din.

Rudyard Kipling

[1] Bring water swiftly.
[2] Mr Atkins' equivalent for 'O brother'.
[3] Be quick
[4] Hit you
[5] Water-skin

THE GREEN EYE OF THE YELLOW GOD

There's a one-eyed yellow idol to the north of Khatmandu,
There's a little marble cross below the town;
There's a broken-hearted woman tends the grave of Mad
   Carew,
And the Yellow God forever gazes down.

He was known as 'Mad Carew' by the subs of Khatmandu,
He was better than they felt inclined to tell;
But for all his foolish pranks, he was worshipped in the ranks,
And the Colonel's daughter smiled on him as well.

He had loved her all along, with the passion of the strong,
The fact that she loved him was plain to all.
She was nearly twenty-one and arrangements had begun
To celebrate her birthday with a ball.

He wrote to ask what present she would like from Mad
   Carew;
They met next day, as he dismissed a squad;
And jestingly she told him then that nothing else would do
But the green eye of the little Yellow God.

On the night before the dance Mad Carew seemed in a
   trance,
And they chaffed him as they puffed at their cigars;
But for once he failed to smile, and he sat alone awhile,
Then went out into the night beneath the stars.

He returned before the dawn, with his shirt and tunic torn,
And a gash across his temples dripping red;
He was patched up right away, and he slept all through the
    day,
And the Colonel's daughter watched beside his bed.

He woke at last and asked if they could send his tunic
    through;
She brought it, and he thanked her with a nod;
He bade her search the pocket, saying, 'That's from Mad
    Carew,'
And she found the little green eye of the God.

She upbraided poor Carew in the way that women do,
Though both her eyes were strangely hot and wet;
But she wouldn't take the stone, and Carew was left alone
With the jewel that he'd chanced his life to get.

When the ball was at its height, on that still and tropic night,
She thought of him, and hastened to his room;
As she crossed the barrack square she could hear the dreamy
    air
Of a waltz tune softly stealing tho' the gloom.

His door was open wide, with silver moonlight shining
    through,
The place was wet and slipp'ry where she trod;
An ugly knife lay buried in the heart of Mad Carew,
'Twas the 'Vengeance of the Little Yellow God.'

There's a one-eyed yellow idol to the north of Khatmandu,
There's a little marble cross below the town;
There's a broken-hearted woman tends the grave of Mad
   Carew,
And the Yellow God forever gazes down.

J. Milton Hayes

INDEX OF FIRST LINES

ADVICE
on the Declamation
of Noble and Inspiring Verse
in Public Places
or for Private Satisfaction

YOU ARE URGED

1. To impress hostile audiences that you are not alone by announcing boldly the author's name in full.

2. To assume an aura of massive confidence. The opening lines should be enunciated unusually loudly with suitably striking gestures (see overleaf), and light-minded persons fixed with a basilisk glare.

3. To excite yourself with Missionary Zeal enough to combat that drably flat Worship of Obscurity preached by our morally depraved and musically debased university literature departments and examination-obsessed schoolteachers.

PRINCIPAL "POSITIONS" OF THE HANDS.

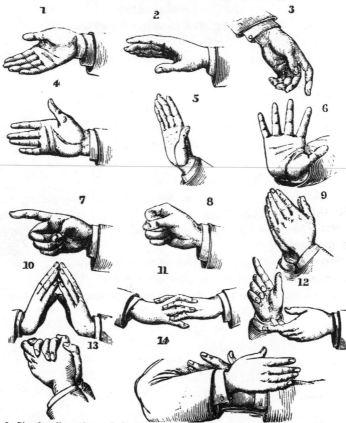

1. Simple affirmation.   2. Emphatic declaration.   3. Apathy or prostration.
4. Energetic appeal.   5. Negation or denial.   6. Violent repulsion.   7. Indexing or cautioning.   8. Determination or anger.   9. Supplication.   10. Gentle entreaty.
11. Carelessness.   12. Argumentativeness.   13. Earnest entreaty.   14. Resignation.